LOOK AND SAY
WHAT YOU SEE
IN THE
COUNTRYSIDE

For my Papa, who loved to spot
and name animals and plants.

S.B.

First published in 2016 by Nosy Crow Ltd
The Crow's Nest, 10a Lant Street
London SE1 1QR
www.nosycrow.com

ISBN 978 0 85763 617 1

The words 'The National Trust' and the oak leaf logo are registered trademarks
used under licence from National Trust (Enterprises) Limited (Registered Company Number 01083105)

Nosy Crow and associated logos are trademarks and/or registered
trademarks of Nosy Crow Ltd (Registered Company Number 7130282)

Text © Nosy Crow 2016
Illustrations © Sebastien Braun 2016

The right of Nosy Crow to be identified as the author and Sebastien Braun
to be identified as the illustrator of this work has been asserted.

A CIP catalogue record for this book is available from the British Library.

Printed in Spain

Papers used by Nosy Crow are made from wood grown in sustainable forests.

1 3 5 7 9 8 6 4 2

LOOK AND SAY
WHAT YOU SEE
IN THE
COUNTRYSIDE

Sebastien Braun

It's a sunny spring day and there's so much to see in the woods!

Can you see . . . ?

fawn

butterfly

bluebell

signpost

Look out for colourful flowers and birds' nests. Can you see any eggs?

How many different flowers can you spot?

daffodil   blossom   blackbird   eggs   tree stump

Some animals live underground, where their homes keep them warm, dry and safe from danger.

Can you see . . . ?

 mole

 log

 spider

 badger

Can you see any baby animals?

fox   roots   ant   worm   rabbit

Rivers are a great place to spot wildlife.

Can you see . . . ?

otter   feather   coot   heron

Many animals live in the water,
but can you see any in the plants
along the riverbanks?

swan   kingfisher   harvest mouse   reeds   cygnet

It's always busy on the farm! With animals in the fields and in the farmyard too, there's so much to explore!

Can you see . . . ?

 cow  horse  magpie  pig

Have you ever
been to a farm?

What did you see there?

tractor   chicken   lamb   hay bale   cat

In summer, meadows are buzzing
with insects and are full of wild flowers.

Can you
see . . .?

cornflowers   cloud   daisy   pheasant

What can you see hiding
in the long grass?

hare   grass snake   poppies   bumblebee   bird of prey

If you take a closer look at plants and flowers,
you'll discover a whole world of creepy-crawlies.

Can you
see . . .?

 centipede  grasshopper beetle caterpillar

Try peeking under a log
to see what's living there!

ladybird   woodlouse   fly   slug   earwig

Trees make good homes for birds because
they can stay up high, away from danger.

How many different
types of bird can you see?

Can you
see . . . ?

squirrel   blue tit   sparrow   woodpecker

cuckoo   birdhouse   nest   chick   swallow

There's always lots going on down by the pond!

Can you see . . . ?

 newt

 frog

 tadpole

 toad

How many ducklings
can you count?

Do you like
feeding the ducks?

bullrushes   dragonfly   duck   fish   lily pad

The hedgerow is full of flowers, fruit and little animals.

Can you see . . .?

honeysuckle snail  blackberries  wren

Can you see an animal sleeping?

Have you ever been blackberry picking?

nettle   rose   dormouse   strawberry   hedgehog

In autumn, it's fun to walk in the forest when the leaves are crunchy underneath your feet!

Can you see . . . ?

 pine cone    mushroom   farmhouse   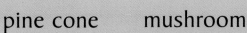 ferns

How many acorns does
the squirrel have?

acorns   mouse   spider web   conkers   stag

Some animals prefer to come out at night-time.
They spend the day resting or sleeping and
only come out to find food when it gets dark.

Can you
see . . . ?

church

firefly

owl

bat

What noise does
an owl make?

full moon   lantern   moth   shooting star   tree

In winter, have a go at making footprints on a snowy walk and look out for wildlife!

Can you see . . . ?

holly berries   robin   snowflakes   pony

Lots of animals will be snuggled up in their warm, cosy shelters, but you might just see some searching for food.

What do you like doing out in the snow?

snowman   mistletoe   paw prints   snowdrop   roe deer